LEADING *in* JOY

FINDING FULFILLMENT AS A SPIRIT-LED LEADER

VENETIA HALSELL

Copyright © 2023 VENETIA HALSELL

Scripture quotations marked (KJV) are taken from the KING JAMES VERSION, public domain. Scriptures marked (NIV) are taken from the NEW INTERNATIONAL VERSION: Scripture taken from THE HOLY BIBLE, NEW INTERNATIONAL VERSION ®. Copyright© 1973, 1978, 1984, 2011 by Biblica, Inc.™. Used by permission of Zondervan. Scriptures marked (NLT) are taken from the HOLY BIBLE, NEW LIVING TRANSLATION (NLT): Scriptures taken from the HOLY BIBLE, NEW LIVING TRANSLATION, Copyright© 1996, 2004, 2007 by Tyndale House Foundation. Used by permission of Tyndale House Publishers, Inc., Carol Stream, Illinois 60188. All rights reserved. Used by permission. Scripture quotations marked (NKJV) are taken from the New King James Version. Copyright © 1982 by Thomas Nelson, Inc. Used by permission. All rights reserved. Bible text from the New King James Version® is not to be reproduced in copies or otherwise by any means except as permitted in writing by Thomas Nelson, Inc., Attn: Bible Rights and Permissions, P.O. Box 141000, Nashville, TN 37214-1000. Scripture quotations marked (ESV) are from the ESV Bible® (The Holy Bible, English Standard Version®), copyright © 2001 by Crossway Bibles, a publishing ministry of Good News Publishers. Used by permission. All rights reserved. Scripture quotations marked (AMP) are taken from the Amplified® Bible, Copyright © 1954, 1958, 1962, 1964, 1965, 1987 by The Lockman Foundation. Used by permission. Scripture quotations marked (MSG) or "The Message" are taken from The Message. Copyright 1993, 1994, 1995, 1996, 2000, 2001, 2002. Used by permission of NavPress Publishing Group. Scripture quotations marked (NRSV) are taken from the NEW REVISED STANDARD VERSION Bible, copyright © 1989 National Council of the Churches of Christ in the United States of America. Used by permission. All rights reserved worldwide. No part of this document may be reproduced or transmitted in any form or by any means, electronic, mechanical, photocopying, recording, or otherwise, without prior written permission of the author.

LEADING IN JOY
Finding Fulfillment as a Spirit-Led Leader

VENETIA HALSELL
venetia.halsell@vhequips.com
www.vhequips.com
@vhequips (Facebook)

ISBN: 978-1-949826-62-3

Printed in the USA.
All rights reserved

Published by: EAGLES GLOBAL BOOKS | Frisco, Texas
In conjunction with the 2023 Eagles Authors Course
Cover & interior designed by DestinedToPublish.com

ENDORSEMENTS

This book is for anyone who aspires to be in a leadership role as well as those who already occupy that space. There is a myriad of helpful topics that I am confident will help you in your journey of leadership.

Venetia Halsell, in her debut book, has brought her vast experience in the leadership arena to the pages of this book. It is a beautifully written book on how to succeed in a leadership role.

Vernita Halsell-Powell
Flag Cluster Leader / TEN Illinois Central Training Facilitator, Apostolic Church of God Liturgical Dance Ministry

ଚ୍ଚର୍ଷ

It is with great joy that I endorse this amazing work of God's gift, Leading in Joy: Finding Fulfillment as a Spirit-Led Leader . This is for every leader and anyone who is called to leadership or to serve God's people in any capacity. Packed with loads of wisdom derived from her personal experiences and research, the author, Ms. Halsell, peels back layers regarding the ministry of leadership, starting at the very beginning, with the question, "What are you called to do?" Without shame or blame, Ms. Halsell empathetically walks you through, step by step, to help identify strategies that assist you in recognizing the difference between a gift, a calling, and a desire. While these three can be very different, Ms. Halsell helps to close the gap between them to find the similarities that assist you with honing in on your journey to successful leadership development, in an effort to move you to genuinely say "Yes" to God's calling to fulfill His assignment—ultimately bringing you to a place where you are *Leading in Joy: Finding Fulfillment as a Spirit-Led Leader*.

Gloria L. Chatman, MA, DTR
Founder and Former Director
Apostolic Church of God Liturgical Dance Ministry

ೋಜ

"*For everyone to whom much is given, from him much will be required*" (Luke 12:48 NKJV).

Venetia Halsell possesses many talents, which she shares freely with others. God revealed her gifts to me, guiding me to place her in a leadership position to rebuild a faltering team. Faith, community, and purpose are the foundations of her leadership style. Venetia is grace personified. Leading by example, Venetia encourages her coworkers to embrace community and service to others. She promotes truth, trust, and relationship building. Venetia drives creative thinking and process improvement. As a true mentor, she recognizes the gifts God has bestowed on others. She challenges her team to accept, develop, and use their gifts to the fullest, all while nurturing their struggles and concerns. I am blessed to personally witness her *Leading in Joy*.

Kristina Guastaferri
Benefits Administrator
MACRC Benefit Funds

DEDICATION

To God, the Creator of all things, who provided the inspiration to write this book. To my loving parents, who are surely smiling down from Heaven at the daughter whose creativity they nurtured at an early age. I am forever grateful for the love and support they provided me through the years. To my son, Kendall, who has so graciously shared his mother his entire life as I pursued my passion and purpose. Thank you, son. I love you dearly!

ACKNOWLEDGEMENTS

To my family (Halsell, Washington, McCree, Powell, and Price), friends, coworkers, and partners in ministry: Thank you all for your words of encouragement, support, and prayers. I am so blessed to have you in my life, and I love you all!

FOREWORD

"He that thinketh he leadeth when no one is following, is merely taking a walk." - John Maxwell

I have known Venetia Halsell for over 30 years. We connected with each other through our love and passion for dancing in the world and again in dance ministry at our home church. In addition, we have served together in other dance ministries and in leadership roles throughout the country. After 30 years, I guess one could say, "We are still kicking, just not as high." While navigating this thing called life and leadership, we have developed a lifelong friendship, and it gives me great pleasure and is an honor to share my insight on Venetia Halsell's first book: *Leading in Joy: Finding Fulfillment as a Spirit-Led Leader*. Leading people is one of the most amazing gifts that someone can be given, but to do this while being led by the spirit of God is on a whole other level.

As a leader and author, Venetia is a servant; she is passionate, gentle, creative, patient, knowledgeable, and wise. She exemplifies the Fruit of the Spirit, which has made her strong and vibrant in the Lord (Galatians 5:22). *Leading in Joy: Finding Fulfillment as a Spirit-Led Leader* is written out of her heartfelt love and dedication to leadership. The power and energy I felt just reading the title sent chills throughout my body.

In today's world, we need strong, vibrant, fervent, and loving leaders who can make an impact on others. Venetia does a superb job illustrating and explaining how a true and passionate leader should lead others. This book covers how to recover and reengage, which is very important for those who have been leading for many years. The reading is captivating, engaging, and reflective as she explains the tools, experiences, and skill sets needed to obtain Spirit-Led results. As a business owner, for me, *Leading in Joy* truly exemplifies the perspective one must have when leading others in business and in life. It is truly a great book to read whether you are a new or seasoned leader, or even with your team as a team-building exercise. There are numerous applicable takeaways, revelations, and self-reflection exercises to enhance your skills personally as a leader. It's not always what you do as a leader, but how you make people feel. How they connect to you is vital to any organization, and this book personifies the steps that are needed to ensure that a leader is Fulfilled, Leading in Joy, and Spirit-Led. Enjoy!

Regina Betton Evans, Co-CEO
Evans & Associates Financial Services Group

Contents

Dedication i

Acknowledgements iii

Foreword v

Introduction ix

Chapter 1: It Starts With You 1

Chapter 2: Competent and Confident 9

Chapter 3: Prepare to Humbly Serve 19

Chapter 4: It's All About the Team 27

Chapter 5: Recovering from Failure 39

Chapter 6: Count It All Joy! 51

Chapter 7: Every Good Tree Bears Good Fruit
              (Matthew 7:17) 56

References 72

Introduction

What brings you joy? Is it spending time with family and friends or engaging in your favorite hobby or sports activity? Perhaps you like to volunteer or mentor youth in your community. How about leading others? It's probably not the first thing that comes to mind when people think of joy. However, you can find great joy in sharing your gifts and talents to help others grow and flourish.

Webster's Dictionary defines joy as an emotion evoked by well-being, success, or good fortune. Joy is also a matter of the heart. It's what you are passionate about. It's an inner peace you feel when you put your trust in God. Many of us serve in leadership in multiple areas: in our jobs, church ministries, and as business owners. So, how does one find joy in their role as a leader? How do you avoid the pitfalls that leave you feeling exhausted, depleted, and joyless at the end of each day? And how do you show up as your authentic self wherever you are leading?

For me, the joy came when I finally understood why I was placed in these leadership roles. Discovering what it really meant to be a leader helped me to understand my purpose as well as my responsibility. I learned to look beyond myself and what I had accomplished and focus on helping others achieve their goals and become the best version of themselves. Sharing my knowledge and skills with others is fulfilling, especially when I see staff members or my students put them into practice. I don't try to create "mini me's"; however, I do get a kick out of seeing them replicate things that I have done or repeat statements that I once told them. I say to myself, "Yes, they are listening!"

I have also learned that you should never underestimate your ability to influence others. Everything you say and do is being watched, scrutinized, and often modeled by those around you. Many leaders, unfortunately, are either not aware of this or don't care. As a result, you still have the "do as I say, not as I do" leadership style of old that simply does not work anymore. People want a leader that they feel good about following. In writing this book, I wanted to bring to the forefront the importance of leaders being introspective, because good leadership starts with you! For example, is your department or ministry experiencing a mass exodus, or is team morale low? It's easy to blame the team for any confusion or dysfunction that they may be experiencing. But how many leaders stop and ask how they may have contributed to it and are willing to accept responsibility? Did you miss the red flags, or did you choose to ignore them? These are all very important questions that leaders need to have answers for. This book will highlight the need for good communication within your team so that you can uncover the root causes of some of these common issues. I firmly believe that most things can be resolved with open and honest communication. When you create an environment where communication is valued, your team will be more willing to share their concerns and give you an opportunity to address them and find solutions before things get out of hand. This level of communication, along with your ability to resolve problems, breeds trust and makes you the kind of leader that people are willing to follow.

Leading in Joy: Finding Fulfillment as a Spirit-Led Leader will challenge new and emerging leaders to view leadership with a different lens. Make no mistake, being a leader is hard work! And being a leader in multiple spheres of influence is even harder. The key is not to separate the roles but to identify your gifts and utilize them in all areas of leadership. In addition, if you are not approaching leadership from a place of service, passion, and purpose, then you will surely miss the joy.

With 30-plus years of experience in leadership roles in the marketplace, ministry, and entrepreneurship, I will share nuggets that I have learned along the way that will transform the way you lead and ultimately transform those you have been given the responsibility of leading.

CHAPTER 1

It Starts With You

Understanding the Call to Leadership

I knew at a very young age that I was destined to be a leader. Why? Because I loved being in front of people. Whether it was reciting a poem I learned in school, entertaining everyone at family gatherings, or teaching my younger siblings everything I had learned in school that day, I was very comfortable being out front. However, as I got older, I began to more fully understand that there was more to being a leader than being in front. Becoming a leader is truly a call that needs to be seriously considered, because your "Yes" will require more from you than you ever imagined.

Now, I'm not trying to scare or discourage you. However, I want you to understand that your ability to lead effectively will not only change your own life but also impact the lives of the people God has entrusted to you.

In his leadership bible, John C. Maxwell tells us that God is the Ultimate Leader, and He calls every believer to lead (influence) others. Maxwell also states in his introduction that "The call to leadership is a consistent pattern in the Bible, and every time God desires to do something great, He calls a leader to step forward." So, what have we been called to do?

Our primary calling is to represent God on Earth and represent Him well. Ephesians 6:20 KJV states, *"For which I am an ambassador in bonds: that therein I may speak boldly, as I ought to speak."* We are called to be an ambassador and bondservant for Christ. We are also called to act justly, love mercy, and walk humbly with God, as stated in Micah 6:8. Mark 16:15 NIV tells us to *"Go into all the world and preach the gospel to all creation."* I Corinthians 7:17 NIV states, *"Nevertheless, each person should live as a believer in whatever situation the Lord has assigned to them, just as God has called them."* God has called us to become the person He has created us to be and to do the things that He has equipped us to do. So, in order to understand what it means to be "called," we first need to understand why we were created.

Scripture tells us in Isaiah 43:21 that God formed us for Himself that we may proclaim His praise. This is the primary purpose for which we were created. Colossians 1:16 NIV says, *"For in him all things were created: things in heaven and on earth, visible and invisible, whether thrones or powers or rulers or authorities; all things have been created through him and for him."* We were created for His glory! Psalm 139:13–14 NIV says, *"For you created my inmost being; you knit me together in my mother's womb. I praise you because I am fearfully and wonderfully made; your works are wonderful, I know that full well."*

We were all created for a purpose. We have a reason for being here. It's up to us to discover what that is if we want to live our lives "on purpose." God uses many means to "call" us. An angel was sent to both Mary and Joseph concerning the birth of Jesus. The burning bush was used to draw Moses into a conversation with God concerning the Israelites. For others, the call came in the form of a dream or vision. In modern times, we hear that still small voice which some refer to as your conscience. Believers call it the Holy Spirit. This "voice" will give you the unction to take action on a situation that could change your life and the lives of those around you but ultimately will bring glory and honor to God.

Now, since we have free will, it is still up to us to either trust God and accept the assignment or disregard it and move on with our lives. There have been many times when I have chosen to disregard because the ask was so big that it scared me. God would give me a vision, which is how He usually speaks to me, and I would ask myself how He expected me to do this. I would start second-guessing myself, thinking that I didn't have the knowledge or skill to pull this off. I would compare myself to other people and similar things that they were doing. Again, being young in my faith at that time, I didn't trust Him enough to know that He would not ask me to do anything that He had not already given me the gifts and talents for. I also had to keep in mind that trusting God also meant that whatever I didn't have, He would ultimately provide, because He was supposed to get the glory out of this assignment and not me.

Even now, I like to reflect on these scriptures when I have those doubting moments or when I feel like I don't have the energy to keep going:

1. II Corinthians 12:9 KJV: "And he said unto me, My grace is sufficient for thee: for my strength is made perfect in weakness."

2. Isaiah 40:29–31 NIV: "He gives strength to the weary and increases the power of the weak. Even youths grow tired and weary, and young men stumble and fall; but those who hope in the Lord will renew their strength."

Now that we understand how God calls us, let's discuss your assignment.

Your Assignment

You have been given the opportunity to lead a group of people either at work or in ministry. You are certain that you have been called by God for such a time as this, and you have a basic understanding of what being "called" means. However, you are questioning how this applies to your role as a leader. Many new leaders dive headfirst into facts, figures, and focusing on the bottom line. Or in dance ministry, we go right for the "5, 6, 7, 8." However, have you prayed and asked God specifically what your assignment is? Why has He placed you in this role? What is it that you are specifically being called to do? Is it about the task or the dance, or are you there to influence and impact the lives of those you are leading?

When you look at leaders like Moses, he was given a specific assignment when God chose him. His assignment was to free the children of Israel out of Egypt (Exodus 3:1–10). Everything Moses did leading up to that moment was for the sole purpose of gaining their freedom. Talk about focus! How awesome it would be to approach your job every day with that same intensity and focus. For example, I remember in one of my supervisory roles, my assignment was to find ways to motivate an underperforming team to begin to meet the standards set by the organization. However, God showed me that in order to do this, I needed to get to the root of the issues that plagued that department, which extended beyond the bottom line. Being clear on my assignment allowed me to not only focus on implementing programs and developing strategies that assisted the team in improving their productivity and meeting their targets, but also to develop an emotionally healthy team that were able to work together to achieve those goals.

In the ministry of dance, our focus is often on learning choreography. However, what if your assignment as the leader is to grow the ministry both technically and spiritually so they can be better equipped to serve and your choreography can transcend to another level of worship? Without clarity of focus and vision, you could miss the mark and ultimately fail to fulfill your assignment. Think about the story of Nehemiah. When he heard that the walls surrounding Jerusalem had been ruined, he fasted and prayed first. Then, God gave him the vision (assignment) to rebuild the wall and provided him with everything he needed, including courage, strength, wisdom, and strategy, to get the job done. As you walk out your role as a leader, always have clarity of purpose and vision. Take the time to seek God for direction. This is vital to the success of your team and their goals. We will discuss this in more detail later in the book.

Your Yes

God has called. You are clear on your assignment. You have said, "Yes, Lord. I hear and obey." Wow! This is huge and often scary. Why? Because you have no idea what lies ahead. In addition, you aren't sure if you even have the skills necessary to fulfill the assignment. I know that's how I have felt many times when I said, "Yes."

Years ago, a young minister of movement approached me and asked if I would be one of her mentors. She had just attended our dance ministry's worship service and said that she had been watching me and a good friend of mine who I affectionately call my partner in ministry. She wanted to know more about the ministry of dance, particularly how to move and lead gracefully, and felt that we could teach her. At the time, my partner and I were the assistant directors for the dance ministry at our church. Now, I was completely surprised by the request, because I had never been asked to mentor anyone and, frankly, I wasn't sure what this new relationship would look like. However, once I received confirmation from the Lord that this was something that I should do, we began what is now a 20-plus-year relationship. I put my trust in Him, and He provided me with wisdom and insight to impart into her as she continued to grow in His grace. She went on to establish and lead her own dance ministry, produce numerous worship services, and mentor other ministers of movement. We may not realize the depth of our knowledge and gifts, but others see it and, most of all, God knows what He has equipped us with.

The Bible gives us many examples of leaders who were hesitant to say yes for fear that they were not equipped for the task. Let's look at the story of Jeremiah, starting with Chapter 1, verses 4–10 NIV. It reads, *"The word of the Lord came to me, saying, 'Before I formed you in the womb I knew you, before you were born I set you apart; I appointed you as a prophet to the nations.' 'Alas, Sovereign Lord,' I said, 'I do not know how to speak; I am too young.' But the Lord said to me, 'Do not say, "I am too young." You must go to everyone I send you to and say whatever I command you. Do not be afraid of them, for I am with you and will rescue you,' declares the Lord. Then the Lord reached out his hand and touched my mouth and said to me, 'I have put my words in your mouth. See, today I appoint you over nations and kingdoms to uproot and tear down, to destroy and overthrow, to build and to plant.'*

God reassured Jeremiah that He would tell him exactly what he needed to say. He told him not to be afraid because He would be with him and rescue him. He went on to tell him specifically what he was being called to do, and Jeremiah went forth as he was instructed. Let God's reassurance give you the courage to go forth, even if it feels scary. Know that He will be on this leadership journey with you as long as you stay focused on Him.

CHAPTER 2

COMPETENT AND CONFIDENT

Identifying Your Gifts and Passion

We all have something that we are passionate about. It's the "thing" that has your heart, your time, and your undivided attention. It's the "thing" that you can't imagine doing without or not being a part of. For me, one of my passions is dancing. I love, love, love to dance and choreograph. I have studied several techniques and disciplines and performed in numerous recitals and productions. However, it wasn't until I was introduced to Praise Dance Ministry that I realized my passion was a gift that God could use for the Kingdom. What does this have to do with leadership? When you are a student of the arts, you develop discipline, perseverance, and the ability to perfect your craft. You are able to measure your success and monitor your progress. All very good traits for a leader to have.

In addition, most artists are creatives, which is a trait that can also serve you as a leader. Your ability to think outside of the box will come in handy when implementing innovative ideas for the organization or your dance ministry. Why is it important to identify your gifts? Because you need to understand what you are naturally good at and recognize those areas that need to be strengthened in order to be successful.

In the corporate world, there is a tool called the Myers-Briggs Personality Type Indicator. According to the Myers & Briggs Foundation, the purpose of this test is to help you identify your personality type from a list of 16 distinctive types. It identifies the differences in how individuals prefer to use their perception and judgment.

The first two types are Extraversion (E) or Introversion (I). Extraversion means you prefer to focus on the outer world, while Introversion means you prefer to focus on your own inner world. The next two types are Sensing (S) or Intuition (N). Sensing means you prefer to focus on the basic information you take in, while Intuition means you prefer to interpret and add meaning to that information. The next two types are Thinking (T) or Feeling (F). Thinking means you prefer to first look at logic and consistency, while Feeling means you prefer to first look at the people and special circumstances. The final two types are Judging (J) or Perceiving (P). Judging means you prefer to get things decided, while Perceiving means you prefer to stay open to new information and options.

Why is this information important? The Foundation states that research shows that people are attracted to careers that allow them to make use of their natural type preferences. The

Foundation also states that when you understand your type preferences, you can approach your own work in a manner that best suits your style, including: how you manage your time, problem-solving, best approaches for decision-making, and dealing with stress.

I have had the opportunity to take this assessment twice in my career. The first time was when I applied for my first management position in my early thirties. The second time was while attending a training conference for my current management position. Needless to say, my preferences have changed over the years. My initial type was ISFJ. This means that in my earlier years as a leader, according to the tool, I was quietly warm, factual, sympathetic, detailed, dependable, organized, thorough, conscientious, systematic, conservative, realistic, caring, practical, stable, and helpful. When I took it again 30 years later, my type had changed. It was now INTJ.

According to the tool, this means that currently I am vision- and meaning-oriented, quietly intense, insightful, creative, sensitive, serious, persevering, and inspiring, and I seek harmony and growth and love language and symbols. What I found to be the most interesting outcome was that I was an introvert. I always considered myself an outgoing person who enjoyed being in social settings. However, I realized that I am an introvert who functions as an extrovert. What does that mean? For me, it means that I am very outgoing in social settings that I am comfortable in. If I know most of the people in attendance, I am extremely social. However, if I am acquainted with only a few people, I tend to sit quietly and observe before I begin to engage. I do enjoy being around people, but I also cherish my alone time. Growing up, everyone thought I was just being moody! Once I realized that I was an introvert, I had to make a conscious effort at work to stay present with my team during times when I would rather have been left alone. In my earlier years of leadership, I remember withdrawing into my office many times when I needed some alone time. While that isn't necessarily a bad thing if you need to get stuff done, I had to be careful not to ignore them the entire day. I found that if I left my office door open, the team knew that I was still available, even if I hadn't left my office for hours at a time.

Understanding that we have some level of all of these personality types within us, it's not unusual due to experience, growth, and maturity that my dominant personality types had shifted. Becoming aware of your personality types allows you to operate in your strengths or make adjustments in those areas that are not natural for you but necessary for you to lead effectively.

In ministry, there's a tool called the Spiritual Gifts Assessment. Similar to the Myers-Briggs Personality Type Indicator, this tool helps you discover your God-given spiritual gifts. According to Lifeway.com, this tool helps you understand where you are spiritually and how God has gifted you. It will help you determine:

a. The depth and strength of how you care for others.
b. Your ability and capacity for getting things done that are critical to Kingdom effectiveness and efficiency.
c. Your ability to understand deep and meaningful concepts that impact yourself and others.
d. How strong or insightful you are at determining what you are facing and what must be done.

There are 25 possible gifts and, based on your scores, you identify the top five. Some of the gifts listed are teaching, creative communication, leadership, encouragement, counseling and faith. I have taken this assessment several times as well. Once when I became part of the leadership team with the dance ministry at my church and then again during my tenure as the site leader for the Eagles Network. My most recent assessment identified my top five gifts in order from highest to lowest as:

Teaching & Faith (tied in 1st place)
Pastor & Administration (tied in 2nd place)
Leadership

What does this mean? The gift of teaching indicates that you are able to understand, clarify, explain, and apply the Word of God to the lives of listeners. Believe it or not, my dream as a child was to be a teacher. It was always another one of my passions to share my knowledge with others so they too can learn and grow. Although teaching did not become my profession in the marketplace, I have been blessed to be able to teach through the Eagles Network and through my business, VH Equips! Praise Dance and Choreography Training Programs.

The gift of faith indicates that you trust God's will and act on it with belief in God's ability and faithfulness. Originally, faith was not in my top five gifts. However, as I began to mature as a Christian, I realized that my gifts were meant to be used outside of the four walls of the church. I began to view my role as a leader in the marketplace as an assignment from God and not just a job. This provided a completely different perspective from what I was accustomed to early in my career and literally shifted the way I approached leadership. Once I realized that I was on divine appointment, I became more prayerful and was able to rely on the leading of the Holy Spirit.

The gift of pastor indicates that you are able to guide, care for, and nurture individuals or groups in the body of Christ. This is a very natural gift for me and falls right in line with my ability to coach and mentor individuals in all of the areas I touch: marketplace, ministry, and entrepreneurship.

The gift of administration indicates that you are able to understand what makes organizations or projects function and have the ability to plan and execute procedures that increase effectiveness. Given this description, you can see why this gift would definitely be an asset to any organization or ministry. The ability to think strategically is essential, and the ability to execute is even more important. How many of you know people who are full of good ideas that never get off the ground because they don't have the ability to plan and execute? I teach a choreography course that shows people how to strategically prepare their choreography. We discuss writing the vision for the dance that God has given them. We talk about writing down movement ideas, garment choices, formation, staging, etc. Several students have shared how valuable this information has been and how it allowed them to consider all facets of creating dance ministry pieces.

Last, but certainly not least, the gift of leadership indicates that you are able to instill vision in, motivate, and direct people to accomplish the work of the ministry. Proverbs 29:18a KJV states, "*Where there is no vision, the people perish.*" All of the great leaders in the Bible not only had to share the vision that God gave them with their followers, but also had to motivate and guide them to fulfill their assignments. I make it a point to share with my team at work the vision or direction of the organization and the role we play in it. This helps us to create goals and determine our contribution to the organization. In ministry, I meet with my TEN team at the beginning of every year. We review the prior year's accomplishments and discuss where we could have done better. We then go on to discuss the vision for the upcoming year. This helps to set the tone for what we need to accomplish and how our ministry and teaching will impact our students.

I am so grateful and blessed to have these as my primary gifts. They have served me well throughout my career and life in general. They have allowed me to operate as my authentic self in both the marketplace and in ministry. I don't need to pretend to be someone that I'm not. If you have an opportunity to take either of these assessments, I recommend you do so. You will find that, once identified, your passion and gifts will be the fuel you need to keep you motivated as you motivate your team.

Become an SME (Subject Matter Expert)

A colleague of mine uses this term with a great deal of pride. She often uses it when she references the members of her team. What is a Subject Matter Expert (SME)? According to Wikipedia, an SME is a person who has accumulated great knowledge in a particular field or topic, which is demonstrated by the person's degree, licensure, and/or through years of professional experience with the subject. This is important for leaders, as your team will look to you for all of the answers, whether you have them or not. They will consider you to be an SME just by virtue of the position you are in.

But what do you do if you don't feel like an expert or if this is your first leadership role? You remain teachable and seek out the training that you need. Whether it's taking a class or attending workshops or seminars, leaders should continuously stay up to date with what's happening in their industries or areas of expertise. Your team is depending on you to pass on that information so that they are able to perform their jobs at a high level. Learning never stops for you.

One thing that many leaders overlook is the value of having a mentor. Mentors are invaluable and vital to your growth process. Align yourself with someone that you admire and look up to. Someone who has the traits and qualities of the type of leader that you would like to become and, most importantly, a leader that you would follow. I have had several excellent mentors both professionally and artistically who helped me when I took on leadership roles in the marketplace and in ministry. They shared their knowledge, wisdom, and time with me, so I felt supported as I navigated this new territory called leadership.

Another way for you to enhance your skills is to seek out those on your team or peers who have the knowledge that you lack. Work collaboratively with those colleagues so that you can glean the knowledge needed to grow in your leadership role. This option is a must when you are recruited from outside of the organization to lead a team. You may have extensive knowledge of the industry, but you will need time to learn the culture of the organization as well as their policies and procedures. Having done this three times in my career, it was critical for me to develop relationships with my peers and seasoned team members in order to get up to speed as quickly as possible.

If you are ever recruited from the outside, you realize very quickly that your newly inherited team will test you to see what you are made of. The sooner you are able to exude confidence and competence, the quicker the team will begin to respect you for your knowledge. Sadly, respecting you because of your position or title is a thing of the past. You will need to prove yourself worthy of the position to gain their buy-in and ultimately their trust.

Engaging Your Faith

As you find your footing, know that your faith will be tested. Doubt will begin to creep in, especially when you face opposition. There will be a time when your team pushes back when you want to implement new initiatives. Maybe your superior shoots down an idea that you thought would be beneficial to the success of your team. Or you overhear your peers saying negative things about you that are not true. Don't get discouraged! Engage your faith! Mark 11:22-24 KJV states, *"And Jesus answering saith unto them, Have faith in God. For verily I say unto you, That whosoever shall say unto this mountain, Be thou removed, and be thou cast into the sea; and shall not doubt in his heart, but shall believe that those things which he saith shall come to pass; he shall have whatsoever he saith. Therefore I say unto you, What things soever ye desire, when ye pray, believe that ye receive them, and ye shall have them."* Take a moment and go to God in prayer. Ask Him for direction and strategies that will move those mountains and give you the clarity to continue to move forward with confidence and great faith.

CHAPTER 3

Prepare to Humbly Serve

Embodying the Characteristics of a Good Leader

I have had the pleasure of teaching sessions on Godly Leadership. One of the ways I like to begin my sessions is to ask the students what characteristics they look for in a leader. By the time that portion of the session was over, the whiteboard would be full! It was clear that people expect a lot from their leaders. Some of the characteristics given were: patient, humble, teachable, knowledgeable, fair, confident, skillful, compassionate, respectful, honest, compassionate, supportive, wise, servant, prayerful, relatable, responsible, mentor, and coach. My next question to the students was, "How likely is it that you will find all of this in one person?" Of course, the answer was "probably not." Given that, I asked what their nonnegotiables were. The majority of the students stated that they must have a leader who is humble, compassionate, patient, prayerful, skillful, knowledgeable, and supportive.

Jesus immediately came to mind because He is the perfect example of a servant leader.

Philippians 2:7 KJV states, "*But made himself of no reputation, and took upon him the form of a servant, and was made in the likeness of men.*" When Jesus began His ministry, He set about doing the work that He was assigned to do. He assembled His team of disciples, trained, mentored and served them, then went out to the masses to preach and teach and serve some more. His final assignment was His death on the cross. Now is a good time to examine why you want to be in leadership. Are you drawn to the title and your new status in the organization? Is it the perceived power that you will have over the people you lead? And let's not forget the increase in salary that comes along with the additional responsibility. Unfortunately, if these examples are your primary reasons for wanting to join the ranks of leadership, you are in it for the wrong reasons.

While all of these things, in most cases, come with the title of Supervisor, Manager, Director, CEO, etc., the title should not define you as a leader. True, authentic leadership is a matter of the heart. If you want to begin to embody the characteristics that I listed earlier, you must have a heart for the people you will be leading. In other words, be prepared to serve them. What does that mean? Your job as a leader is to use your gifts and talents to help the organization meet their goals, but you are charged with helping your team members meet their goals as well. You want them to become the best versions of themselves so that one day they will be able to advance within the organization, if that is their desire.

I confess that in the early stages of my career, I had my eye on becoming a supervisor. I started my career as a claims processor trainee right out of college. The supervisor that hired me was a wonderful mentor and taught me everything she could. I progressed through all of the levels available as a claims processor and soon became bored with the day-to-day routine. Like most employees who get to that point, you have a decision to make: Do you stay and settle into the mundane, or do you aspire for something more? For me, the next step was supervision.

Needless to say, when I was given the opportunity to become a supervisor at the age of 27, I really thought I was ready. Surely, my processing skills were all I needed to be successful in this new role. How wrong I was! I found out very quickly that being a leader was less about what you can do individually and more about how you can empower your team to produce collectively. Hence, you must be willing to share your knowledge and expertise with them, while simultaneously learning new leadership skills yourself. So, if you don't enjoy engaging with people on a daily basis, leadership is not the job for you!

Jesus was among people during his entire ministry on earth. You always found him in a crowd. Whether it was in a synagogue (Matthew 12:9, Matthew 13:54, and Mark 1:21) or on top of a mountain (Matthew 5:1–48), his ministry was all about how he could serve the people he encountered.

Leading by Example

Have you ever heard the saying "do as I say, not as I do"? Do you have someone in your life that loves to give you advice but doesn't seem to live it out themselves? How likely are you to follow their well-intentioned advice? Not likely or, at most, reluctantly. As leaders, you must realize that your team is watching everything you say and do, so it is important that you are modeling the behaviors that you want to see in your team. You become their role model, whether you want to be or not.

According to Julia Martins in her article "How to Lead by Example," one Asana leader states that leading by example is the difference between saying, "You can do this" and "We can do this together." Though the support and encouragement in the former is great, the latter builds connection, camaraderie, and trust. People who lead by example actively demonstrate their team's value by carrying some of the weight themselves. She goes on to say that this leadership style fosters high levels of engagement and buy-in, because leaders actively demonstrate that they are invested in their team's initiatives.

This leadership style comes naturally for me, because I genuinely enjoy jumping in and getting my hands dirty when deadlines need to be met or if we are in the midst of a major project. I still allow my team to utilize their skills by not taking over; however, I let them know that I am fully invested and available when they need me.

There are several examples in the Bible of how Jesus led by example. In John 13:4-15 KJV, Jesus provides an example of servanthood by washing his disciples' feet after the last supper. When Peter begins to question what Jesus is doing and why, Jesus answers him in verse 15, "*For I have given you an example, that ye should do as I have done to you.*"

There are many more scenarios where leading by example can influence positive outcomes. One that personally comes to mind for me was a simple change in language in emails. I worked for an organization where internal emails rarely began with a greeting (Good morning or Good afternoon) or a closing (Thank you, Sincerely, or Have a good day). The sender would just launch into the content of the email. However, once I started sending emails with greetings and closings, I noticed that most team members, as well as some of my peers, began doing the same. This may seem like a small thing, but it makes for a more personable interaction with the reader.

Another instance is when you need to implement or discuss a policy or procedure that you don't necessarily agree with and that you know is not going to be well received by your team. If you have instilled a culture of respect, you will set your personal feelings aside and do your best to impress upon the team the need for this new policy or procedure and how it benefits the organization or enhances their ability to complete their tasks. Use facts, details, and a positive attitude to combat any negativity from the team. You can even share that this wasn't your first choice (a moment of transparency), but that you are confident that together, the team can make it work. This shows that you are able to agree to disagree and still be respectful of your leaders. After all, managers and supervisors all report to someone! If your team see that you can submit to your leadership, they are more likely to do the same. I love this quote on page 1261 of The John Maxwell Leadership Bible. It says, "Jesus teaches every leader that the first person you lead is you. We earn the right to lead others when they see us lead well in our own lives."

Sacrifice Required

There is no truer statement that applies to this topic than the scripture found in Luke 12:48b. I like both the NIV Bible translation and The Message translation. The Word of God says:

a. *"From everyone who has been given much, much will be demanded; and from the one who has been entrusted with much, much more will be asked."* (NIV translation)
b. *"Great gifts mean great responsibilities; greater gifts, greater responsibilities!"* (The Message translation)

I like to quote this scripture to my newly promoted leaders. Why? It's not to scare them, but to help them understand that this leadership journey will challenge them to their core. It will often have them second-guessing why they chose to do this. However, if they stay focused on the reason why they chose to be a leader, they will do fine. Again, let's talk about that heart of service. Leaders understand that their teams need them to not only lead but also provide feedback, impart knowledge, coach, and mentor them. The key is figuring out how to do all of this while managing your day-to-day tasks. This can prove to be quite daunting, especially for new leaders. I remember my early days of leadership. I had no idea how to juggle all of this, and my time management skills were horrible. I had stacks and stacks of papers all over my desk! When my boss asked me for a document, it would take me several minutes to unearth it. It was so embarrassing!

Nowadays, technology has moved us more toward a paperless environment. But, back in the day, the health-care industry was 99.9% paper. I also need to add that when I became overwhelmed, procrastination would set in. Because I am the type that likes to check things off my list, I would do the simpler tasks first to feel like I had accomplished something. However, this did not bode well for the more complicated tasks that were often the ones that needed to be done first. Not to mention that when my team had questions or needed me to guide them through a process, they were met with a cranky, irritable, and stressed out supervisor. I quickly realized that if I didn't reach out for help, I was going to drown, and fast!

I reached out to my manager, who already knew I was struggling. She arranged for me to have training on time management techniques and helped me to prioritize my tasks. I also learned how to delegate tasks that didn't need supervisory-level expertise. This not only helped me stay afloat but also freed up my time so I could spend the time needed to work with my team. Notice that my manager didn't take anything away from me; she simply showed me how to best manage my time. The responsibilities of a leader are vast, and it becomes your responsibility to figure out how to handle it all. Whether you do it all yourself or choose to delegate some portions of your tasks, the outcome is still your responsibility. If you see yourself in this scenario, the best advice I can offer is to reach out to your superior and ask for help. If you don't feel comfortable with this because you think it might expose your flaws, let me just say, your boss already sees it.

Now, if you have a trusted peer or a mentor as suggested earlier, they can help you through this process. Very often, as in my case, earlier bosses are your mentors. I was able to develop relationships with my mentors that provided me access to their knowledge, skills, and expertise. They also knew that I was interested in advancing, so they made sure to expose me to situations that would continue to help me grow. We will talk more about the impact of mentors in the next chapter and how you will be able to allocate this valuable time in order to mentor members of your team.

Chapter 4

It's All About the Team

A Heart for the People

I recently read a quote by Simon Sinek on minimalistquotes.com which said, "Leadership is not about being in charge. Leadership is about taking care of those in your charge." Servant leaders understand that they are in a position to impact, influence, empower, and inspire their teams. Therefore, they understand that it is important to build relationships with each member of their team. Having a heart for people means that you will show compassion when needed. You show grace when mistakes are made, and you have a tremendous sense of responsibility for your team and serve them with passion and commitment.

John 15:12-13 NIV says, *"My command is this: Love each other as I have loved you. Greater love has no one than this: to lay down one's life for one's friends."* God wants us to love one another the way He loves us. In order to love someone, you need to be in a relationship with them. I am repeating this because many leaders fail to see the need for this. Now, I am in no way suggesting that you need to be bosom buddies and share all your innermost secrets. However, I am suggesting that you get to know what makes your employees tick. What are their goals and aspirations? What motivates them? What do they enjoy about their jobs? Do they have suggestions for improvements or efficiencies? When you begin to engage in these types of conversations, your employees will feel like you genuinely care about them. People are more willing to follow leaders that make them feel valued and heard.

What if you have someone on your team that is particularly difficult? Your first instinct might be to ignore them or keep them at arm's length. Why? Because it's easier to shy away from someone whose personality or temperament is challenging. However, you need to love them just like everyone else. I can tell you from experience that those personalities tend to be a defense mechanism that is hiding past hurts and disappointments. By taking the time to get to know them, you just might be the one who can break through those barriers and reveal a smart, competent person who had simply shut down due to poor leadership.

Communication is Key

To be an effective leader, you must be an effective communicator. When I say effective communicator, I am referring to all forms of communication: verbal, nonverbal, and written. Have you heard the saying, "it's not what you say, but how you say it"?

So much damage is done by leaders who don't know how to communicate effectively. Proverbs 18:21a KJV says, "*Death and life are in the power of the tongue...*" Words are powerful! They have the ability to uplift and encourage or tear down and discourage. That's why it is important for leaders to think carefully before they speak. Choosing your words wisely can prevent hurt feelings and misunderstandings. It doesn't matter if you say them verbally or written in an email; the wrong choice of words can have disastrous consequences. And remember, once those words are out there, you can't take them back.

So, how do you become an effective communicator? Start by actively listening. After all, God gave us two ears and one mouth for a reason. Active listening allows you to focus on what is being said and also gives the speaker your undivided attention. Wikipedia defines active listening as the practice of preparing to listen, observing what verbal and nonverbal messages are being sent, and then providing appropriate feedback for the sake of showing attentiveness to the message being presented.

This form of listening conveys a mutual understanding between speaker and listener. Active listening makes the speaker feel heard, and you have an opportunity to provide support and encouragement. This form of communication helps to build trust with your team and shows them that you are genuinely interested in what they have to say. One key factor in active listening is for you to pay attention to the nonverbal cues being demonstrated by the speaker. It's important to see if they match what the person is saying or if there may be something that is being withheld during the conversation. We'll talk more about nonverbal cues later in this section. Another key point is that active listening forces you to concentrate on what is being said instead of thinking about how you want to respond. This also prevents you from interrupting the speaker before they finish their thought. This often occurs when the topic of conversation centers around unpleasant feedback, such as poor performance or lack of adherence to policies. Emotions are often high and defenses are up. Active listening can help you remain calm and respond in a professional manner, even when your team member is upset.

Now let's talk about your delivery. As I mentioned earlier, it's not always what you say, but how you say it that makes the difference. According to the article "The Three Basic Communication Styles" found on page 28 of Jane's journal on the Habits for Wellbeing website, there are three communication styles you need to be aware of: (1) Aggressive Communicator: Are you a direct, no nonsense communicator that likes to get right to the point? Are you sometimes seen as hostile or defensive with no consideration for others? Then, you are an Aggressive Communicator. This communication style can be very offensive and hurtful to the person on the receiving end. This communication style is not ideal for anyone, but especially not for a leader. (2) Passive Communicator: Are you someone who is unable to articulate your position or feelings, which causes you to harbor resentment and anger? Do you allow others to speak on your behalf? Then, you are a Passive Communicator. This communication style is considered emotionally dishonest, as you never communicate how you really feel. A leader who is a Passive Communicator will be emotionally draining to their team. The team will never get a sense of how their leader feels about anything and, therefore, trusting their leader will be an issue.

In addition, since the leader doesn't express their true feelings, they will eventually lash out when things aren't going well and create what could become a hostile environment. (3) Assertive Communicator: Are you able to articulate your thoughts and feelings while respecting the other person's thoughts and feelings? Are you able to relate to others? Then, you are an Assertive Communicator. This communication style is the most effective of the three. It allows room for people to express differences with mutual respect and trust. This is the style that I most identify with. I am able to be firm when needed, without damaging my team in the process. Directives can be given in a way that leaves people whole, whether they disagree with it or not. The use of tone and nonverbal cues is an essential part of this type of communication, which will be discussed below.

Now that we have identified the most common types of communicators, we should discuss why tone of voice is an important part of these three communication styles. We know that tone of voice means the way you speak to someone and how you use your voice to make a point. We also know that the wrong tone can cause your communication to be misinterpreted and misunderstood. Let's take the Aggressive Communicator. Their tone is often formal, serious, matter-of-fact, and coarse. This tone lacks warmth and empathy, which are important traits for good communicators. The tone of the Passive Communicator is typically soft spoken, apologetic, hesitant, and indirect. This tone makes the leader appear to be unsure, emotional, and weak. This leader can be prone to emotional outbursts, because they bottle up their emotions until they reach a breaking point. Again, they are unable to effectively articulate their concerns. Now, there are several examples of tones that can be effectively used to enhance your communication skills. Since we have already established that the Assertive Communicator is the most effective, below are some of the tones these communicators use:

Friendly Tone: Sincere, kind, pleasant, approachable, nonthreatening.

Humorous Tone: Lighthearted, funny, amusing, comical.

Conversational Tone: Refers to written communication utilizing simple words that you would use in everyday conversation. An informal style of writing.

Motivating Tone: Excited, high-pitched, fast-paced.

Respectful Tone: Polite, humble, kind, warm.

Try incorporating a few of these tones in the delivery of your verbal and written communication. You will find that your messages will be well received and clearly understood by the recipient.

Nonverbal communication is the last piece of this very important subject. This form of communication utilizes eye contact, gestures, facial expressions, posture, and body language to help convey your message. When communicating with others, you want to ensure that your nonverbal communication matches what you are saying. If you are communicating a lighthearted message but you have a scowl on your face, the listeners will be confused by this mixed messaging. If you are someone who uses your hands when you talk, be careful not to wave them uncontrollably or aggressively, as the listener may feel intimidated or threatened. Do make eye contact when communicating; however, be careful not to stare so intently that you cause the other person to feel uncomfortable.

Now, if someone is speaking to you, nonverbal communication is just as important. If you want to let the speaker know that you are open and engaged in the conversation, i.e., actively listening, try not to fold/cross your arms, as this is often seen as a defensive posture. Smile and nod occasionally to acknowledge that you hear and understand what they are saying.

Communication at best is tricky but can be mastered with practice and intention. Knowing your audience and being able to adjust your communication style will go a long way in making sure your message is clearly understood and not lost due to incorrect grammar, tone, and/or body language. If you struggle in this area, help is available through a plethora of workshops, seminars, and courses offered by local colleges and universities as well as private training companies. They all offer some type of communication and/or speech course. My first introduction to public speaking was in a speech class I took in undergrad. I not only learned how to write different styles of speeches but also how to present them. I enjoyed it immensely and took a second speech class the following semester. I realized that being an effective communicator adds credibility and allows you to interact with all levels of people with confidence.

Vision and Goals

"*Where there is no vision, the people perish*" (Proverbs 29:18a KJV)

In his Introduction to Proverbs on page 762, John Maxwell tells us that good leaders see beyond what followers do and bigger than followers do. Leaders must think, envision, and plan well into the future. The primary difference between a leader and followers is perspective. What does this mean? It's the way a leader thinks and perceives reality and then acts accordingly. Why is it important for a leader to have vision? The leader needs to be able to see and understand the direction of the organization. Where does the vision originate? If the leader is part of an organization, the vision is given by the CEO or administrator. They have likely pulled all of the frontline leaders together and discussed the direction for the organization for the upcoming year(s). Once the leader is clear, their job is to clearly communicate that vision to their team. This communication is usually done with energy and enthusiasm, so that the team can be motivated to take the necessary action to ensure the vision comes to pass. Once the vision has been cast, the leader begins to strategize and develop goals and benchmarks for the team, so that expectations are set and their progress can be measured. This approach moves the team and ultimately the organization closer to manifesting the vision that was shared.

Goal setting is an important part of this process. As stated above, it allows the leader to set clear expectations and monitor progress. However, goal setting is equally important for the members of the team. Most people want to know if they are meeting expectations, and they want to do a good job. If there is no clear direction, they have no guide and find themselves floundering, unsure if they are meeting the expectations of the organization.

Setting goals provides a space for constructive feedback on a regular basis, so team members don't have to wait until annual review time to find out that they were not performing. Regular feedback also allows for course correction and retraining, if needed. This will allow for continued growth in the areas where there may be a skills gap or deficit. While goal setting can be tedious and time consuming, especially when you include the frequent feedback meetings, I find this to be the most effective way to grow your team. It fosters an ongoing one-on-one relationship with your team members and shows a genuine concern for their growth within the organization. This is the perfect lead into our next topic of coaching and mentoring.

Coaching and Mentoring = Legacy

"Give instruction to the wise, and they will become wiser still; teach the righteous and they will gain in learning" (Proverbs 9:9 NRSV).

I love how John Maxwell addresses the topic of leaders leaving a legacy. He states on page 1218, "When all is said and done, your ability as a leader will be judged by how well your people and your organization did after you were gone. Your lasting value will be measured by succession." He goes on to say, "Being a leader has a price; being a leader who leaves a legacy has an even greater price. When you work to create a legacy, your life is no longer your own. That's why it's so important to know what you are willing to give up so that others can go up." Whew! Take a moment and let that sink in. I mentioned in an earlier chapter that sacrifices would need to be made as leaders give so much of themselves. As you can see, creating a legacy will require you to spend time coaching and mentoring those on your team that have the potential to go higher. If you were fortunate enough to be mentored, you understand the value of this type of relationship and how it impacted your career. It's only right for you to reach down and do the same for those that will come behind you.

How does the mentor/mentee relationship begin? For me it begins with a conversation. Since your role is to help groom this individual, it's important to know what they want and what they are aspiring to do. In turn, you can set the expectations of what needs to be accomplished during your time together. In addition, we have check-ins along the way to ensure that progress is being made.

In the case of the mentee I mentioned earlier, we initially started with movement. She wasn't very strong in dance technique, so we began to work on that aspect. We showed her how to effectively present ministry by utilizing her space and clarifying her movements. From there, we began to consult regarding issues that would arise as she was leading her dance team. We would provide her with ideas and strategies on how to address these issues from a biblical perspective and provide support when needed. We always made ourselves available to her when she needed us. And, to this day, we are there for her whenever she calls.

In the marketplace, my mentoring is done on an as-needed basis with my direct reports. We are in constant communication regarding the day-to-day activities in the department. I provide consistent feedback throughout the day; however, we also meet on a quarterly basis. We review their goals and discuss outcomes. I set clear expectations based on their needs and provide correction and guidance as needed. This approach works well due to proximity, because I see them on a daily basis. However, it's also the most exhausting approach, because you see them every day! You are constantly carving out time to pour into them while trying to stay on top of your own responsibilities. Let me be clear that this is not at all a complaint, as I enjoy what I do. I'm just pointing you back to the effort and sacrifice required to be an effective mentor and leader.

As a mentor, your goal is to help mold and shape your mentees so they become the best versions of themselves. Ultimately, you want them to gain the knowledge and skills necessary to go to the next level, whether that's in an organization or in ministry. Your influence should be evident in how they carry on in your absence and even after you have moved on. That's leaving a legacy.

CHAPTER 5

RECOVERING FROM FAILURE

The Cost of Poor Leadership

If I had a dollar for every horrible boss/leader story I've heard, I'd be a rich woman. Fortunately, I have been blessed to be able to work for great bosses. Were they perfect? No. But they were humble enough to acknowledge their shortcomings and look within, instead of blaming those around them. Those leaders knew that they were a work in progress just like the rest of us. However, in this chapter, we are going to talk about the downside of poor leadership and how it affects the team as well as the organization when leaders don't see themselves as contributing to the problem.

You have an insecure leader who can't seem to acknowledge the exceptional work of their bright team members. In fact, this leader often takes the credit for their work or ideas. This leader also belittles anyone who has more knowledge than they do in order to make themselves look smarter or more important. They see those team members as a threat to their position of authority. Unfortunately, this leader will never admit their shortcomings. Instead of working alongside a more knowledgeable team member who could assist them, they would rather suffer through a project alone and risk submitting a subpar product. The downside with this type of leader is that the team cannot trust them. The team members feel used, frustrated, overlooked, and devalued. They will eventually shut down, check out, or leave, because their innovation and creativity is being blocked by the insecure leader.

The task-focused leader has no concern for their team. It's all about the work, whatever the cost. This leader often has few to no people skills and shows no empathy when sensitive situations arise. This leader has no coaching or mentoring skills, and when a team member asks a question or needs direction, the leader will often tell them to leave the task with them and they will do it themselves. This leader is so busy doing "stuff" that they have no time for their team. In turn, the team feels ignored and abandoned with no support. The downside with this type of leader is that the team doesn't grow, because the leader doesn't share their knowledge or provide any additional opportunities for their team members to learn and grow. As a result, when opportunities become available within the organization, people who report to this type of leader are not equipped to move up the ladder.

The conflict avoidance leader never confronts anything. They hide in their office or cubicle as confusion and chaos erupts all around them. The team will attempt to share their concerns regarding their coworkers and the atmosphere that has been created. However, this leader will do little to rectify the situation. They won't talk directly to the individuals causing the confusion, but rather address it globally to the entire team to avoid confrontation. This strategy leaves the team feeling helpless and gives unintended power to the ones who are intentionally wreaking havoc within the department. Most people cannot thrive in this type of environment, so they eventually check out and leave the team or organization.

I could go on and on with many more scenarios, but the bottom line is, horrible bosses and leaders leave collateral damage. They have not taken their position of leadership seriously and don't realize that they have left a trail of hurt, wounded, and angry people behind. Once those leaders move on, it makes it difficult for the next one that comes along. The new leader often has to work through years of neglect before they can move forward with department goals. So, how does a leader move forward with a wounded team? Let's start by identifying the problem.

Identify the Problem

If you are fortunate or unfortunate enough to inherit a wounded team, you likely won't know the source of the problem. As their new leader, be careful not to blame them for the turmoil that they experienced and may still be fostering upon your arrival. Your job or, dare I say, your assignment, is to get to the root of the problem. How do you do that? You start by building relationships with your team members. Your first order of business will be to meet with them both individually and collectively. Try to get them to open up about what they are feeling and what they think they need in order to move beyond the hurt. Active listening will be key here, which is why I stressed early on that communication is so important. Also, let them know what your plans are for the department and that you are there to help and support them. Make a list of all of the concerns addressed, whether you think they are valid or not. This will help you begin to prioritize the items that will provide the most impact once they have been addressed and resolved.

Once the team sees that you are taking an interest in their concerns, it will go a long way toward building their trust. However, be sure to keep your conversations with them confidential and only share with those that need to know, such as HR if they are to support you with finding solutions. I can tell you from experience that this will not be an easy process. It can take months, even years, to chip away at the problem. That's why you will need to follow the leading of the Holy Spirit as it guides you through this process.

Many of us do not have a degree in psychology or psychiatry, so these conversations will often unearth feelings and behaviors that are beyond your capacity to deal with. The Holy Spirit will give you the words to say and provide you with the guidance needed to pass on to that team member, whether it's a referral to speak to someone who is equipped to deal with their situation or a matter of you offering to pray for them. You will find yourself turning to God for wisdom and strength in these matters. In addition, if your organization offers behavioral health services, don't be afraid to suggest those resources to your team as well as using them yourself. Tackling these issues can be emotionally draining, and as empathetic leaders, we need a space to release those burdens as well.

Finding Solutions

You have your list of "problems" before you. Where do you start to find solutions? What resources are available to you? The answers will depend on the depth of the problems identified. Let's look at some examples.

Problem: *My ideas are always ignored. Management doesn't take my input seriously.*

Solution: As a new leader, you likely have plans to make some changes within the department. Start by asking for the team's input. After all, they are currently doing the job, so they may have ideas on how the work can be done more efficiently. Take all of the ideas into consideration and determine which ones are more in line with the goals and vision of the organization. Let the team know that you will implement one or two of them on a trial basis and check back within 30 days or so to see if you are achieving the desired outcome. For those ideas that may be too far off the mark, explain that while you appreciated their contribution, it's not something that can be done at this time. That team member will likely appreciate the fact that you acknowledged their idea, even if it couldn't be used.

Problem: *It's not my fault that I can't meet my production and quality targets. I can only do one or the other.*

Solution: Find out why the team member feels like they can't accomplish both. If there is a skill gap, provide the necessary training. If organization or time management is the issue, work with them to organize their day and look for efficiencies. Many people add unnecessary steps to the process that become huge time wasters. Be prepared for some pushback, as they may initially see this as micromanagement. However, stick with it. The time investment will eventually pay off, and you will see their productivity and quality of work improve.

Problem: *There's an unofficial leader in the department who is doing everything they can to work against you. There are some team members who want to work with you but are being encouraged not to. They have come to you with their concerns, as it is creating an uncomfortable environment for them.*

Solution: There's a reason why this person is the unofficial leader. They have probably been with the organization for a long time and are therefore very knowledgeable when it comes to the job tasks and the organization as a whole. However, for some reason, they have not transitioned into the ranks of management and may be harboring some bad feelings because of it. They could have even been passed over when the organization decided to bring you in. The team respects this person for their knowledge, and they obviously have a great deal of influence over the team. This will be a tall order and require great patience and composure on your part.

Don't view them as the enemy! You need this individual on your side, because they can become your greatest ally if dealt with correctly. They have knowledge, skills, and influence, so tap into that. Bring them into the conversation. Ask for their input. Show concern, even if they don't show the same for you. However, do establish boundaries. Do not tolerate disruptive behavior, and be sure to address it at every turn and be consistent. Again, it may take some time to win them over. However, if they refuse to come along, they may decide to leave the department, or you may wind up managing them out. I am always hopeful for a more positive outcome, but unfortunately, it doesn't always turn out that way.

We haven't talked much about the disciplinary side of leadership, but know that it comes with the territory. There are rules and guidelines that everyone is required to follow, and there should be repercussions for those who don't. As a leader, you must not ignore these indiscretions, as it will be detrimental to the well-being of the team. There is nothing worse for team morale than someone getting away with something that the rest of the team knows is inappropriate. I always tell my supervisors that consistency is key. I know that it's uncomfortable and sometimes combative, but it's very necessary in order to maintain compliance within your department. It also provides the team member with an opportunity to course-correct and shows the rest of the team that you are serious about everyone adhering to the rules.

Learn the Lesson

As you may have noticed by now, this chapter dealt with recovering from the failures of other leaders. Yes, you will make your share of mistakes along the way. However, my hope was to show you how to avoid some of those pitfalls. For those of us who were hired into leadership positions from outside of the organization, it's highly likely that we will encounter one of the scenarios that I have presented. Having experienced the above scenarios multiple times in my career, I have to say that I failed miserably the first time. However, I am someone who recognizes their mistakes, learns the lesson, and vows to do better the next time. Fortunately, we serve a God of second chances. So, when presented with these scenarios again, I was better equipped to deal with them, which resulted in much better outcomes. Here are the five most important lessons that I learned:

1. *Pray without ceasing!* What does that mean? Keep God top of your mind every day, all day. Why? Because He is the source of your strength. And you will need plenty of that to deal with the challenges of leading a wounded team. There will be days when their words will cut you to the core. Have you ever heard the saying "Hurt people hurt people"? This is so true, and the hurt will manifest as you try to work through their pain and gain their trust. They will lash out at you, blame you, defame you. But God! With His strength you will be able to stay focused on your assignment and press through. He will allow you to see that you are not the problem but the solution and not to take it personally. I call it developing a thick skin.

   Trust me, this is easier said than done. There were many days when I wanted to respond to my team members' accusations in an equally negative way, because I felt like I had to defend myself. How dare they say those things about me when I am just trying to help them! But as I began to mature in my faith, humility enabled me to approach these situations from a different perspective. As I mentioned in an earlier chapter, love on them even if they don't love you back.

2. *Keep the lines of communication open, and develop those relationships.* Being able to effectively communicate in this atmosphere is critical. Having one-on-one's with each team member gives you an opportunity to get to know

them and them an opportunity to get to know you. Why is it important for them to know who you are? Because in a world where everyone is out for themselves, the team needs to know that you are genuinely interested in their growth and development. They need to know that you are there to listen, guide, and redirect as needed. I never saw the value of this type of relationship until much later. It doesn't mean that I was aloof or unapproachable; I was so busy doing "stuff" that I didn't invest the time needed to properly nurture those relationships. I did have a few people in my inner circle that I interacted with more frequently than others—mostly my direct reports. However, I did not fully extend myself beyond that point.

3. *Keep those conversations confidential.* Nothing will ruin your credibility more than sharing information that was told to you in confidence. Now, understand that as a leader there may be things that you are obligated to report to your superiors. When that happens, you need to make sure you inform your team member that you may need to share this with higher-ups due to the nature of the information. But, if it doesn't need to be reported, then please don't share it! What you should do is ask what they would like you to do with this information. Again, some of these conversations can be heavy, and you don't want to become the dumping ground or the complaint department. Your goal is to find solutions. I tell my team that they should expect me to take action if they bring an

issue to my attention. They are now okay with it because they know that I can address it without divulging the source of the information. They also know that I will fully investigate the allegation before I take corrective action. That was the primary lesson for me. You need to be very careful when people bring issues to you. You have to take the time to validate the information and confirm whether or not it is factual. Unfortunately, there are pot stirrers in every department, and you never want to falsely accuse someone of doing something based on what someone else told you. Utilize all of your resources to verify and confirm. I have had to go as far as informally interviewing staff to see if there was any truth to the accusation being presented. I guess I can add super sleuth to my résumé!

4. *Do something!* As mentioned above, God has placed you in this position for a reason: to fulfill his purpose on Earth. Scripture tells us in Joshua 1:9 ESV, *"Have I not commanded you? Be strong and courageous. Do not be frightened, and do not be dismayed, for the Lord your God is with you wherever you go."* Being a leader is not for the faint of heart. The bigger the assignment, the scarier it is. The greater the challenge, the more it will require from you. However, you must go forth and do! As you are looking for solutions that will help move your team as well as the organization or ministry forward, don't be afraid to try new things. As my coach used to say, nothing grows in the comfort zone. One of my least favorite phrases is "because we've always done

it that way." Well, maybe it's time to shift! Maybe it's time for a new thing! Now, let's be clear, I am not a believer in tearing down foundations. If your team or ministry was built on a solid foundation, there is no need to tear it down and start over. You simply continue to build from there. Effective leaders are change agents! Organizations are always looking for leaders who come in with a fresh perspective and new, innovative ways to achieve the desired results. Whether it's an increase in performance metrics or a shift in the organizational culture, make sure you are the leader that initiates or at least contributes to that change.

5. *Give yourself some grace!* Mistakes will happen. After all, we are human with weaknesses and frailties. Don't be too hard on yourself when things don't go according to plan. Take a deep breath, assess the situation, make the necessary adjustments, and try again. Change takes time and effort, and you may need to try multiple things and utilize multiple resources before you get it right. The lesson here is don't get frustrated and give up. Keep trying! The team is counting on you. The organization or ministry is counting on you. But most of all, God is counting on you!

CHAPTER 6

Count It All Joy!

Back on Track

For this section, I want to shift my focus back to ministry. Why? Because for me, the same leadership principles and strategies apply whether I am leading at work or in the ministries I'm affiliated with. We all know that life happens to all of us, and it is so easy to get distracted and sidetracked from what you have been called to do. Frustration will quickly set in, and you want to retreat, change course, or give up altogether.

Every year I have the opportunity to choreograph a graduation ministry piece for our students. I am always very prayerful regarding the song selection, and it always seems to fit where the students are in that season. Last year, God gave me a song that I had only heard once before. The song was powerful, and I immediately downloaded it and played it every day for weeks. When God confirmed that this was the song to be used, I initially resisted. It was a big song, and I wasn't sure I could do it justice. However, operating out of obedience, I began to write the vision as He gave it to me. What He showed me was that I wasn't supposed to choreograph this alone. I was to use the other members of my team to contribute choreography, as well as some of the students. The lesson here is that just because you can doesn't mean you should. If there are other creatives on your team, give them room to create! God may give you the vision, but that doesn't prevent you from collaborating to bring it to life. God was so specific with His instructions that He laid it out for me right down to who would be responsible for each section of the song.

Now that I was feeling really good about this assignment, I began to share with the rest of the team. However, as we began to move forward, life started happening! I really felt that we were under attack from all sides! One by one, the students were getting sick. I had to pull in the team to learn the choreography as a backup. The rehearsals weren't going well, and I was really getting nervous. Now, I understood that this was the trick of the enemy, and he comes for us every year when we are working on these ministry pieces. It's how he distracts you from bringing God's word forward.

Well, it almost worked this time! I had made the decision that this piece could not go forth, because it would not be ready in time. I started looking for alternative song choices that were shorter in length and easier to choreograph. However, God clearly spoke to me and said that I needed to get back on track and stick with the vision He had given me. Changing course and giving up on this was not an option. So, I put my trust in God and, with the team, continued to execute the vision. We didn't know that there were people who would be attending the graduation that needed to receive that message. But God did. It reminds me of the scripture in Habakkuk 2:3a KJV which says, *"For the vision is yet for an appointed time, but at the end it shall speak, and not lie..."* Don't give up on your assignment. It may not be easy, and it might even be scary, but God will give you everything you need. Stay focused, work through the challenges, and get back on track.

When It All Comes Together

Now that we have overcome every obstacle and challenge— we have prayed and cried and communicated until there was nothing left to say—it's time to experience the joy. Everything that you have been working toward leads to joy when it all comes together.

Let's go back to the choreography project mentioned earlier. The ministry piece turned out beautifully, and it was more powerful than any of us could ever have imagined. The people who attended the graduation were blessed and God was glorified. Imagine if I had not stuck with it and tried to present something different. It's the same with any assignment that God gives you. There is a feeling of great satisfaction when you can look back over the process and see how it all unfolded. I am always in awe of how God works these things out.

Let's revisit the scenario of the unofficial leader. Imagine this person now being your strongest ally and joyfully working alongside you instead of against you, because you have put in the work to nurture that relationship. You planted seeds, prayed for them, and watched God change their heart and mind. I don't know about you, but that transformation would bring me great joy!

How about the team member who doesn't feel heard? One day this employee makes a suggestion that is not quite viable. However, with further communication and a few tweaks, you are able to implement the idea, which results in improved efficiencies, thereby saving money for the organization. You now have an employee who is not only proud of their suggestion, but totally engaged and ready to contribute even more ideas. The bonus is that their excitement has rubbed off on their peers, because you gave them recognition for their idea. The atmosphere in the department has completely shifted for the better, and now other team members are contributing. Taking the time to really listen, offer your expertise, and provide recognition ultimately caused a positive shift in your department. That would make me a very happy leader!

There are several scriptures in the Bible that talk about joy coming after you have overcome your circumstances. Psalm 126:5 KJV says, *"They that sow in tears shall reap in joy."* Nehemiah 8:10c NIV says, *"Do not grieve, for the joy of the Lord is your strength."* Psalm 30:5b KJV says, *"Weeping may endure for a night, but joy cometh in the morning."* In each scripture, we see that you may have to go through some things before you find your joy. There can be great joy in leading others; you just need to be patient and wait for it.

The Fruit of Your Labor

Psalm 128 AMP says, "Blessed [happy and sheltered by God's favor] is everyone who fears the Lord [and worships Him with obedience], Who walks in His ways and lives according to His commandments."

Psalm 128:1-2 NLT says, *"How joyful are those who fear the Lord—all who follow his ways!*

You will enjoy the fruit of your labor. How joyful and prosperous you will be!"

Well, there's that word "joy" again! God tells us that when we follow His ways, when we operate in obedience to Him, we will be blessed. And as a result, we get to enjoy the fruit of all our hard work. And on top of that, we will be joyful and prosperous! I don't know about you, but this scripture is so encouraging. No one wants to think that all of their efforts have been for nothing. You want to know that your "Yes" has yielded results that you can be proud of and that the favor and blessings that God has provided you has overflowed onto your family, friends, and those around you.

CHAPTER 7

Every Good Tree Bears Good Fruit (Matthew 7:17)

God is using you for His special purpose -
To shine His light,
To share His love,
To shape His people
Dayspring

How You Lead Matters

Make no mistake, your leadership has the potential to change lives. However, how you lead determines whether that change is for the better or worse. When done right, your influence can be the catalyst that propels others into fulfilling their God-given purpose. I love how the Bible uses the symbolism of trees to describe growth and life. From the beginning, man was to take care of the garden and provide what's needed so it can grow. I see leadership in the same way. God has entrusted us with these individuals, and it is up to us to give them what they need to grow and thrive. When this happens, you, being the good tree, will produce or bear good fruit. The testimonials below are a wonderful example of this. Let's examine how these individuals describe their respective leaders and the influence they have had on their lives.

Testimonial #1

S. Galindo states: *"The definition of a successful mentor is (leader's name). This leader's mentorship has a positive impact on her mentees through active listening and providing guidance during difficult or stressful times. She plays a vital role in supporting the well-being of her mentees. She is passionate about helping others. She creates strong social ties, encourages a growth mindset, and promotes a learning culture within the organization. She helps her mentees reach their goals and encourages them to be the best version of themselves. She is a great communicator. She articulates in a way that is easy to understand. She shares advice, knowledge, and experiences in a seamless manner. She is honest, provides candid feedback, and is very patient, understanding, and encouraging without passing judgment. Her leadership approach is effortless. She guides mentees to answer questions rather than telling the answer. This leader is truly meant to be a great mentor.*

In closing, I want to express my gratitude to (leader's name) for being such a great mentor in my life and career. She has helped me change the trajectory of my career. I'm truly thankful for all the support and your commitment to my success. Thank you for always inspiring me to put my best foot forward, even when I didn't feel like I belong or have doubts. Your constant reassurance has always helped me navigate through tough times. Thank you for your constant advice, time, and insight. You have made me a better person in both my life and career. I'm truly grateful for all the support and knowledge you have given throughout the years. Most importantly, going above and beyond for me. Thank you for believing in me!"

Well, there's a lot to unpack here. The first thing S. Galindo shares is that this leader is a mentor. She states that her leader provides candid feedback, which is so important in order for a person to grow. But, not only does she provide candid feedback, but she also does it with patience and understanding. You never want to tear people down. You can correct them without destroying their self-esteem. She goes on to list numerous characteristics that describe this leader and expresses her gratitude for the leader investing their time and energy in her development. If you recall, in an earlier chapter we talked about the characteristics people look for in a leader. Do any of these look familiar?

Testimonial #2

S. Magana states: "I met (leader's name) in 2019 at a job interview. She had a warm, welcoming spirit and a bright smile. Throughout the interview, I felt the presence of the Lord around her. Currently she's my manager, and she does a great job managing me. She's my mentor who tells it like it is and *guides me in the right direction. She puts God first, teaching me to do the same and to learn from my mistakes. I am so thankful to have her in my life. She's truly a child of the most high God."*

This leader's light is definitely shining! S. Magana recognizes that there's something different about this person. Never dull your light for anyone. Matthew 5:16 KJV tells us, "Let your light so shine before men, that they may see your good works, and glorify your Father which is in heaven." It also appears that this leader is a mentor as well.

Testimonial #3

L. Powell states: *"If you need an ideal example of an effective leader and how to become one, then look no further than (leader's name). Under her leadership, I have learned that listening to those that look to you for guidance will help you quickly gain trust and acceptance. Ultimately, the greatest leaders are extraordinary listeners. Also, constantly being aware of situations and circumstances helps you to make wise decisions for those that follow your lead. She countlessly reminds me that everyone learns differently. With that knowledge, she challenges me to discover strategies that work with those individually while simultaneously and collectively getting everyone to the same goal. She's effectively helped me to not use accusatory language while giving negative feedback. This has helped me tremendously, as my words are carefully crafted to make those receiving the feedback take ownership of any mishandlings. I could go on and on, but I must mention this one thing: If (leader) sees a potential skill set in an individual, she makes it her duty to lock in and help to develop it until it becomes second nature. Most often, without the individual noticing it happening. She has personally done this for me. Her involvement in my growth has allowed me to achieve success much sooner than I expected and has granted me to receive blessings beyond measure. Thank you, (leader), for being a prominent mentor. You are heaven-sent!"*

Notice that there is a recurring theme: These leaders all function as mentors to these individuals. It's that mentorship that has helped to shape and grow them. You also notice similarities in the words used to describe these leaders. They are good listeners and good communicators, and they are attentive and seem to know what each person needs in order to succeed.

Testimonial #4
R. Wade states: "During my eight years of dance ministry, this leader has become my mentor, Sister in Christ, and friend. To begin, I should say that I came late in life to the dance ministry with no professional training whatsoever. (Leader's name) is one of the main people that has helped mold me into a confident, skilled, and bold dance minister, where once I was timid, untrained, and uncertain. So, the first thing to know is she inspires trust.

She is a special kind of leader; in my opinion she leads effortlessly and smoothly, if that makes sense. By that I mean I never got the feeling of "being led" or any manner of overbearing activity. Yes, I knew I was following her leadership and instruction, but the way she leads, I felt happy to follow her. I truly believe that, especially in ministry of any kind, you must be able to live before your students in a manner that is upright and uplifting. Leading by example is not just words, but it is what I see in (leader's name). So, for a person with a strong personality like mine, I need to see who you are following as I follow you. (Leader's name) follows Christ. She has inspired trust, not only in her leadership, but also in myself and in my relationship with God.

She has taught me principles in the ministry of dance that I find myself applying in life. Her leadership is also highly CREATIVE. She finds ways to demonstrate lessons she is teaching. For example, in the "Ark of the Covenant/Temple" method she used, which gave us an experience of actually being there in the temple. I must be clear here, she has not only taught me dance movement; she has taught biblical principles as they relate to dance and life in general. The curriculum she's brought before us follows a consistent level and flow of cohesion. She inspires participation in a classroom teaching session. You never feel that your answer will be shot down, but encouraged towards correction.

In my experience, her leadership skills, teaching methods, and welcoming personality are among the most excellent of all teachers. I believe that countless people in our lives make up the whole person that we are. I don't mind saying I am a better dance minister and a better person. I am so thankful that her leadership has been a part of my life.

This leader functions in ministry as a leader and teacher. It appears that she is an SME in this area, and this individual talks about how much she has learned from her. Again, it is important to hone your skills so that you are able to share what you have learned with others. As stated earlier, learning never stops for you. This leader also shares one of the same traits as others previously discussed: her ability to lead seems effortless. I can only attribute that to a high skill level and/or experience.

Never underestimate the power of your influence. How you lead truly matters! These testimonials show how these leaders were able to impact the lives of these individuals.

CONCLUSION

Discovering what it really means to be a leader will help you to understand your purpose as well as your responsibility. Understanding your call, your assignment, and identifying the gifts that God has placed within you will assist you as you prepare to humbly serve the people that God has entrusted to your care. Strive to embody the characteristics of a good leader as stated in the book, and lead by example.

Leadership also requires that you become an effective communicator, that you share vision and goals with your team and serve as a coach and mentor to help them learn and grow. Remember that your influence will stay with them and be your legacy long after you move on. Be willing to acknowledge your mistakes and identify problems. But, most importantly, find solutions and learn the lessons that allow you and your team to keep moving forward.

My prayer for you is that this book has given you a different perspective on your role as a leader, and that you will turn to God for guidance and direction as you lead others. I know that being a leader can be very rewarding, but it's not without its challenges. However, with God's help, you will be able to fulfill your God-given assignment and ultimately experience leading in joy!

NOTES AND REFLECTIONS

Use these pages to jot down your leadership challenges, thoughts, and possible solutions using the principles taught in the book.

_____

_____

_____

_____

_____

_____

_____

_____

VENETIA HALSELL

NOTES AND REFLECTIONS

LEADING IN JOY

NOTES AND REFLECTIONS

VENETIA HALSELL

NOTES AND REFLECTIONS

NOTES AND REFLECTIONS

VENETIA HALSELL

NOTES AND REFLECTIONS

LEADING IN JOY

NOTES AND REFLECTIONS

SOURCE DOCUMENTS REFERENCES

John C. Maxwell, The Maxwell Leadership Bible, Revised and Updated, Lessons in Leadership from the Word of God, Second Edition

The Myers & Briggs Foundation, myersbriggs.org

Simon Sinek, minimalistquote.com

Lifeway.com

Wikipedia

Julia Martins, article, "How to Lead by Example"

Jane Taylor, "The Three Basic Communication Styles", habitsforwellbeing.com

Dayspringquotes.com

www.ingramcontent.com/pod-product-compliance
Lightning Source LLC
Chambersburg PA
CBHW071202090426
42736CB00012B/2420